LADYBIRD COLORING BOOK

CRYSTAL
COLORING BOOKS

ISBN-13: 978-1546835769
ISBN-10: 1546835768

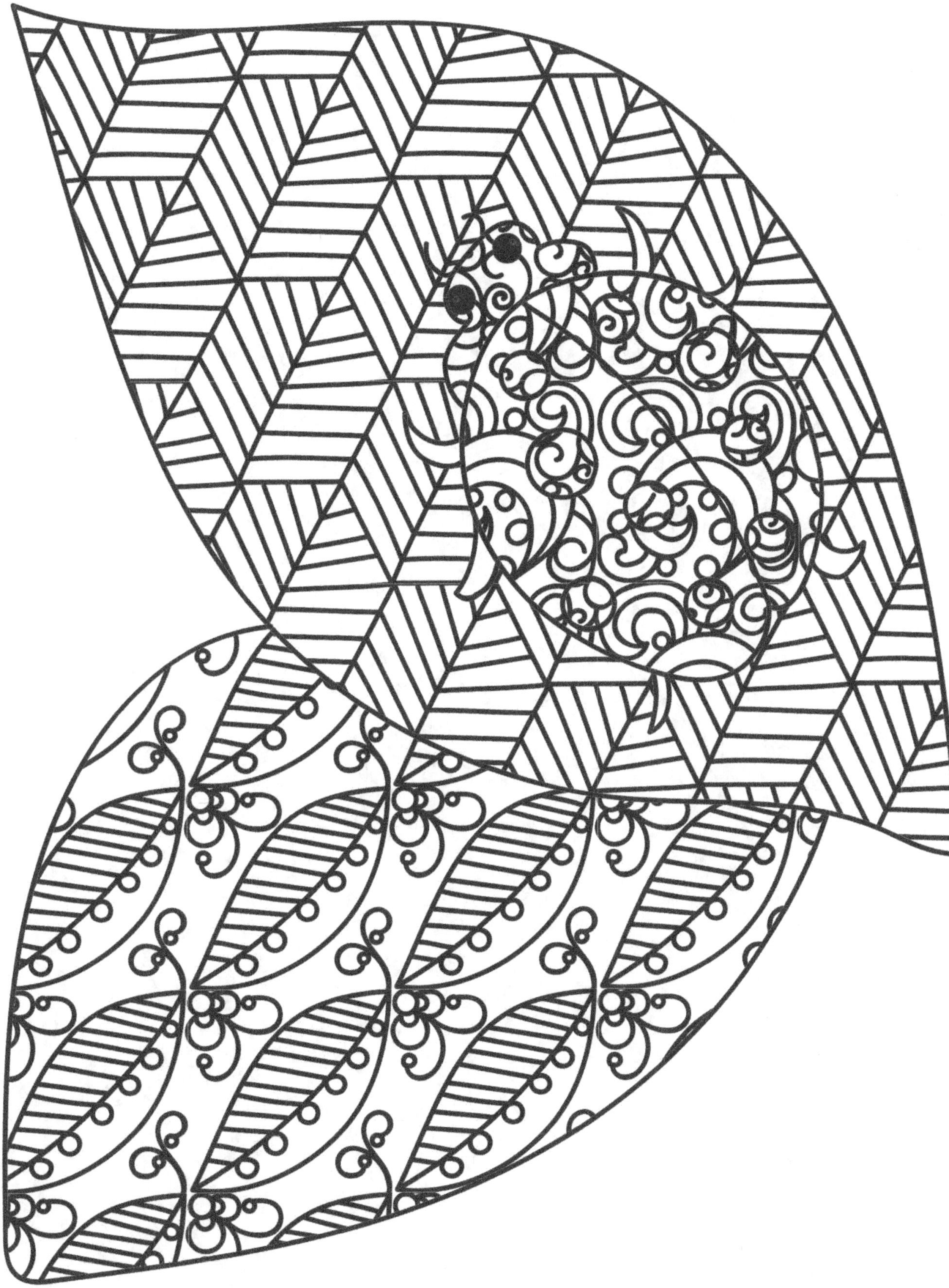

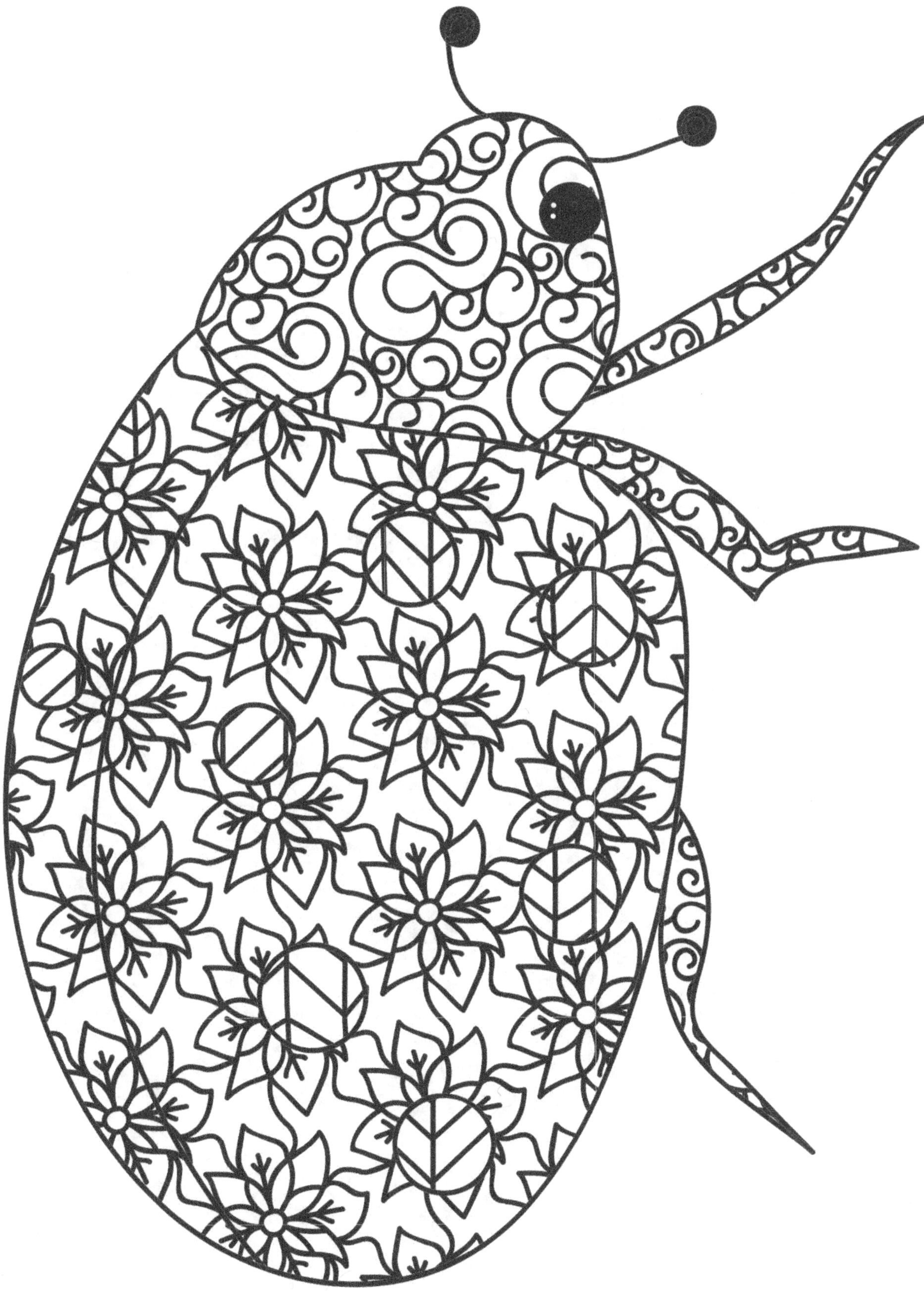

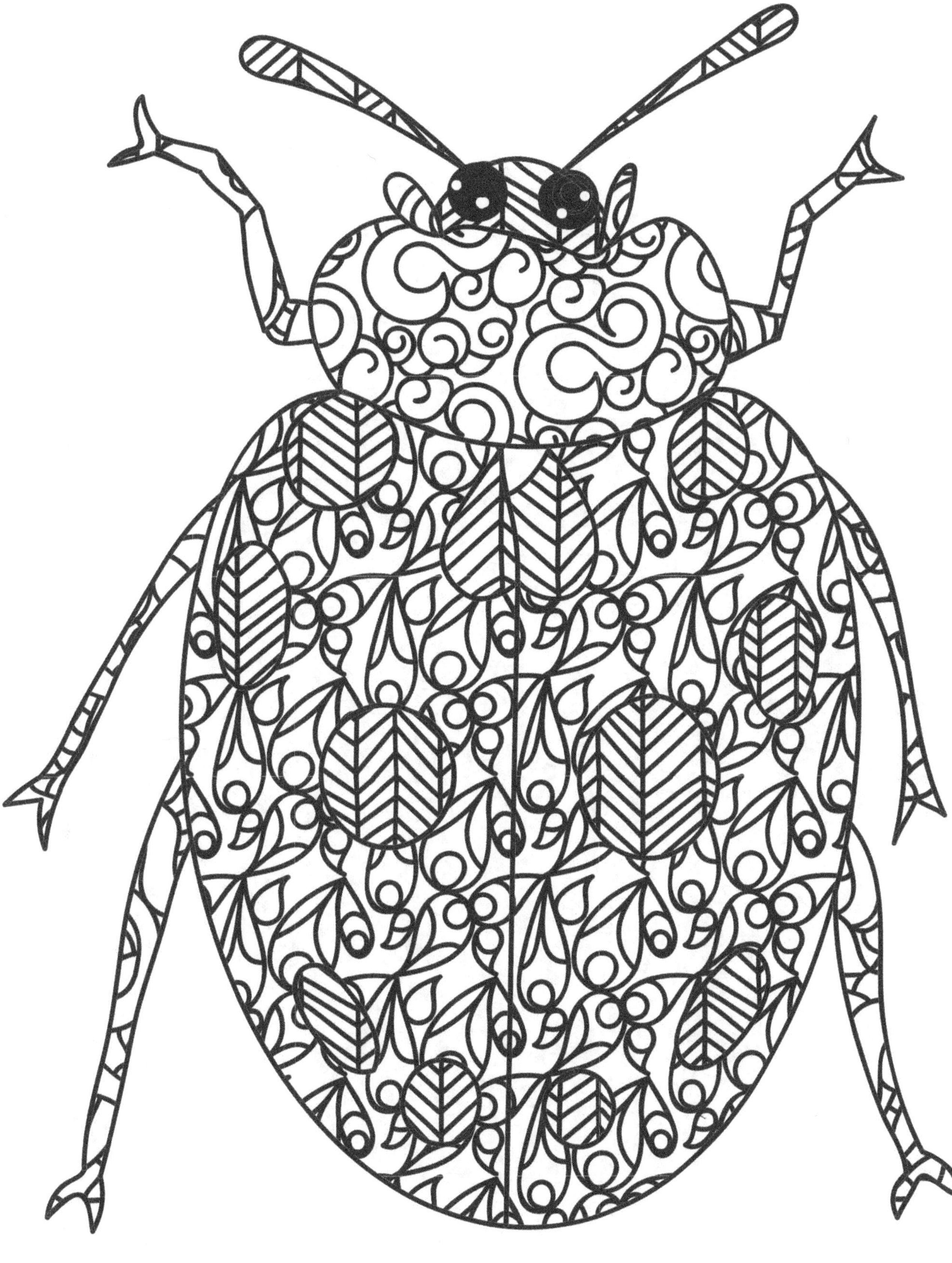

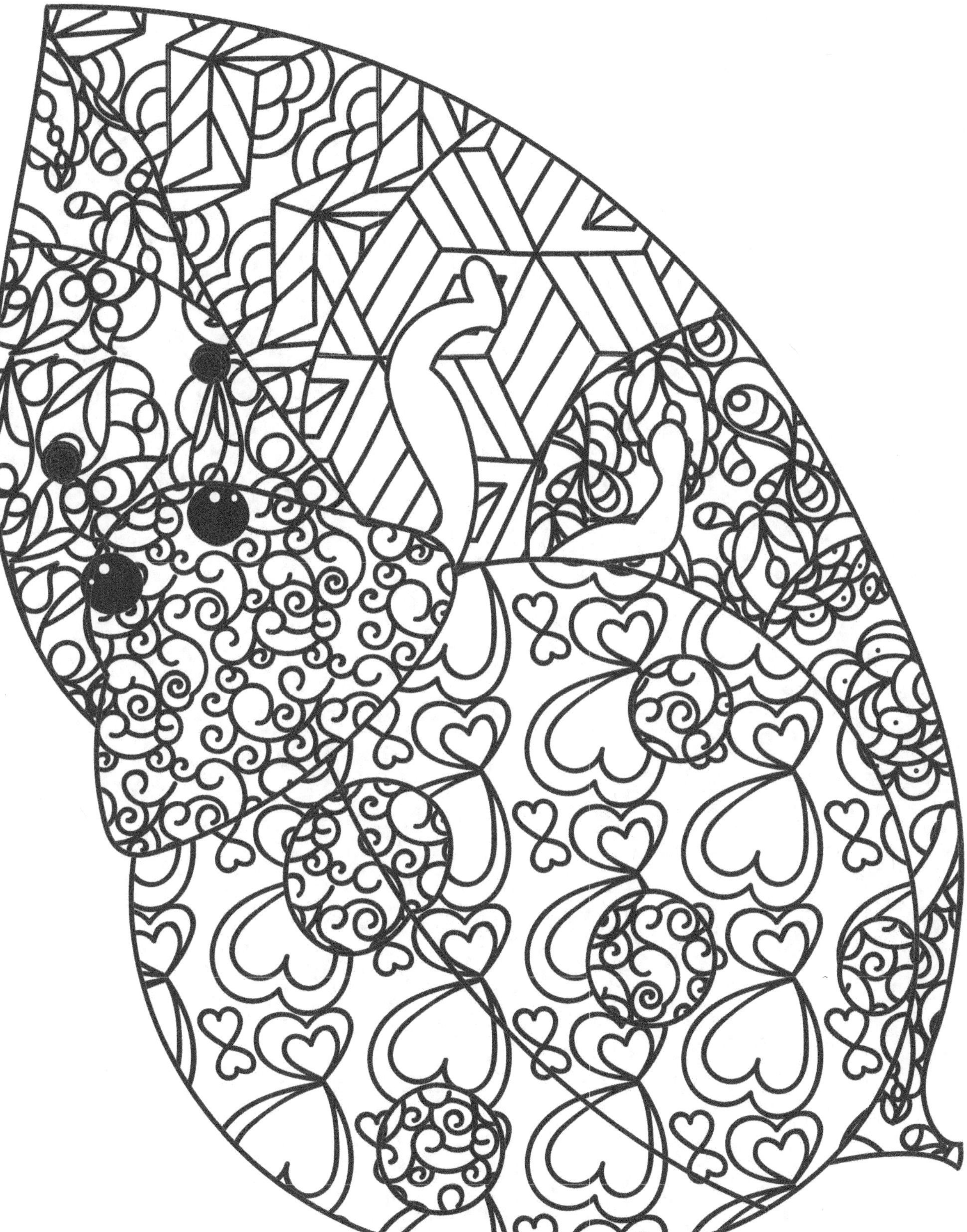

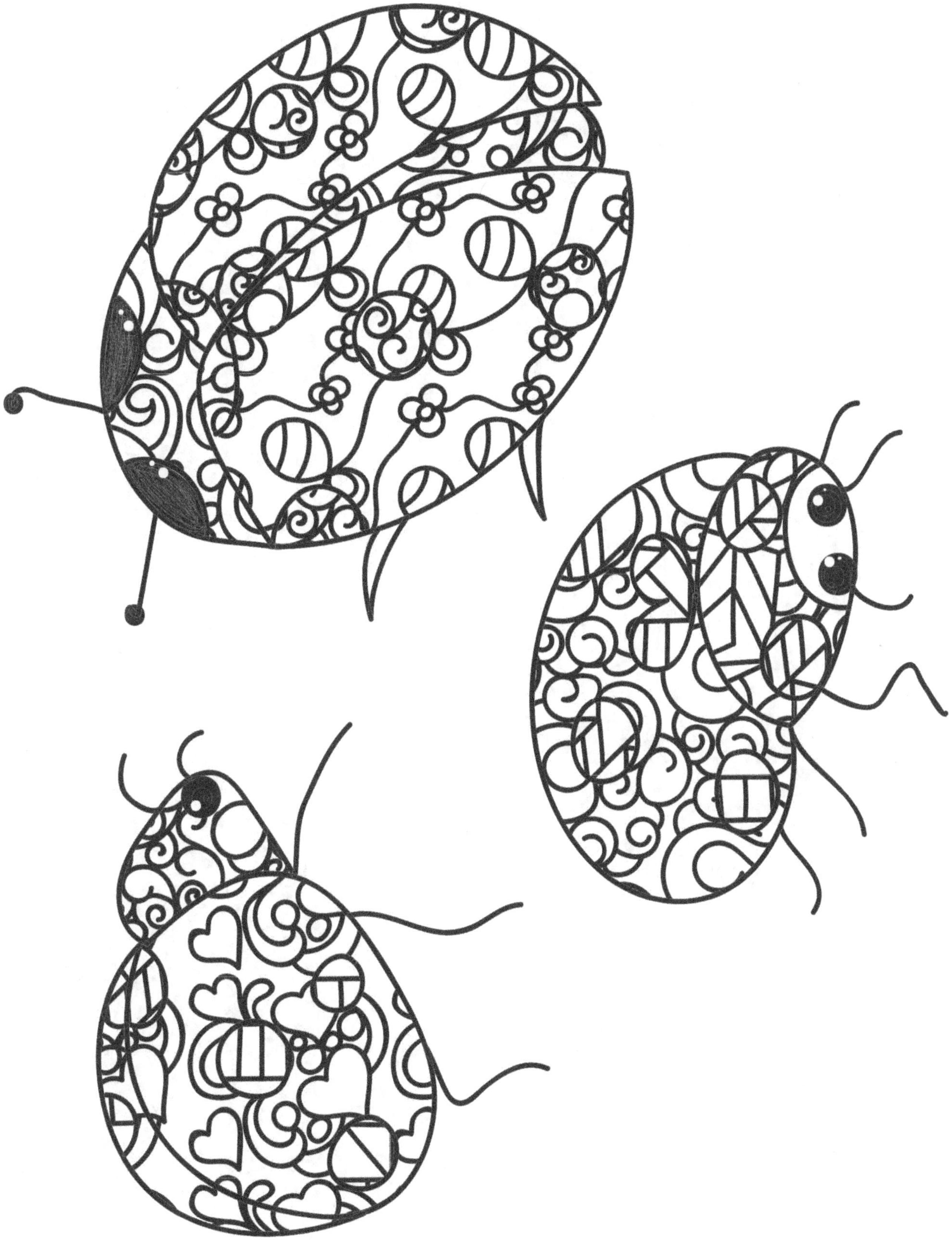

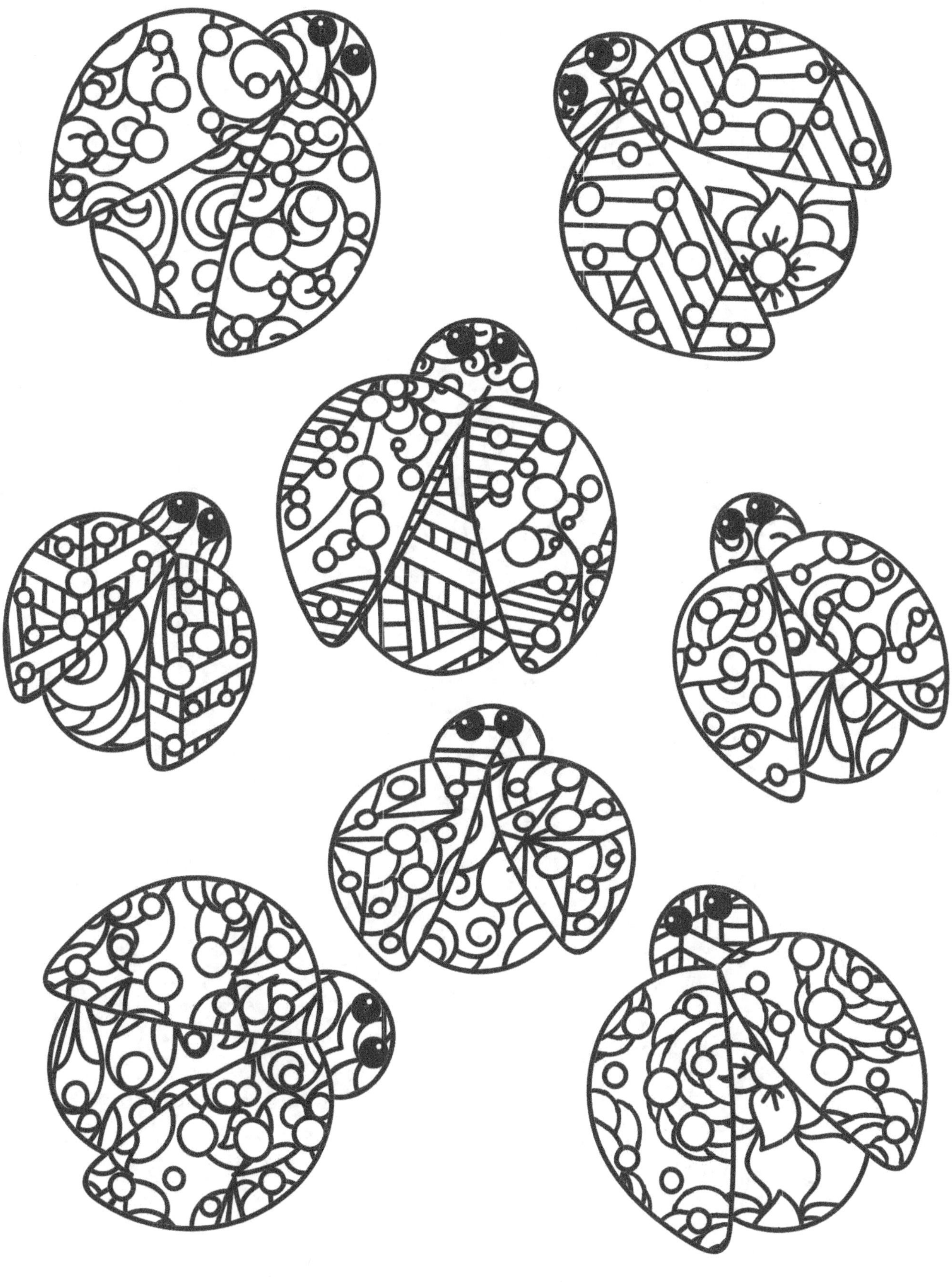

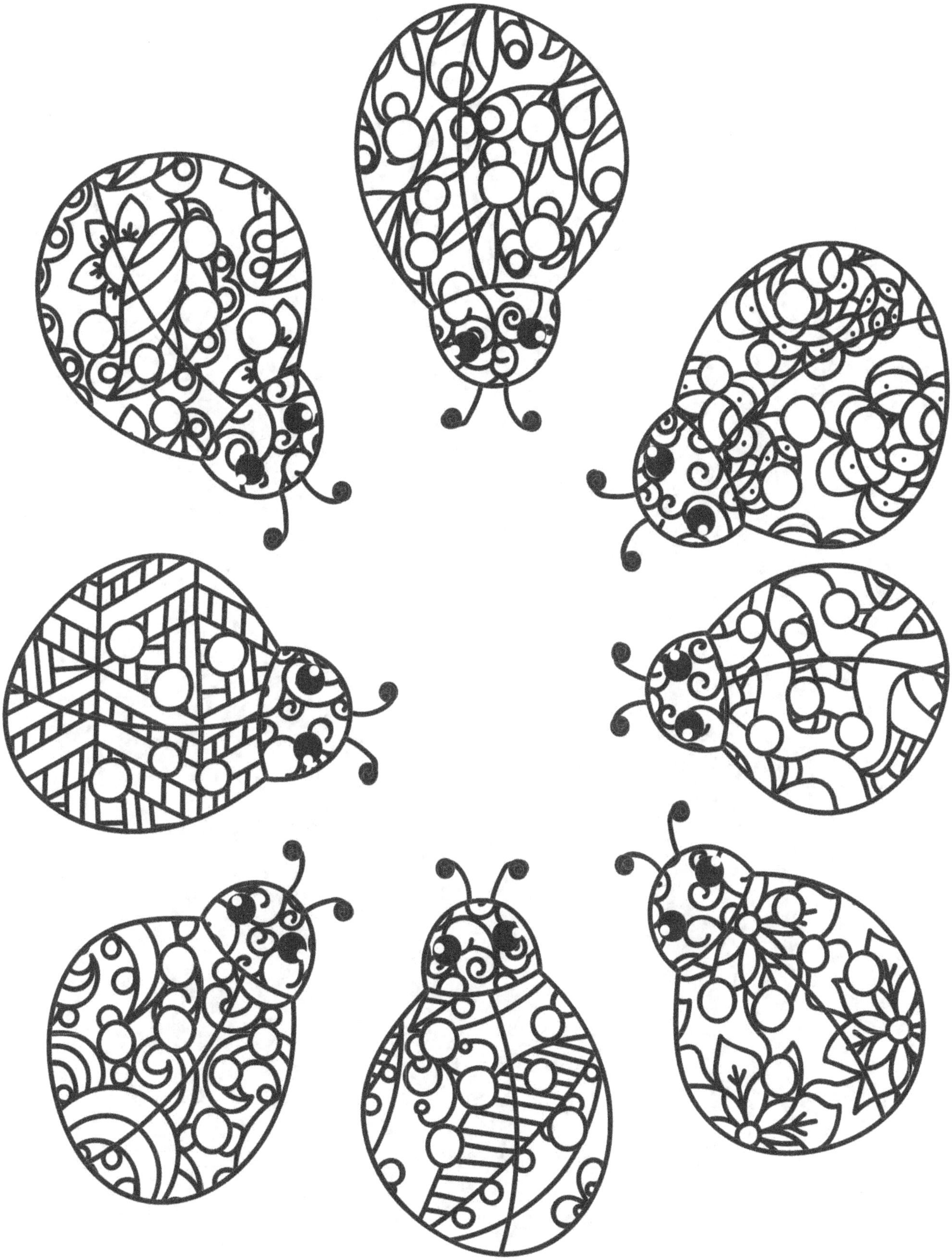

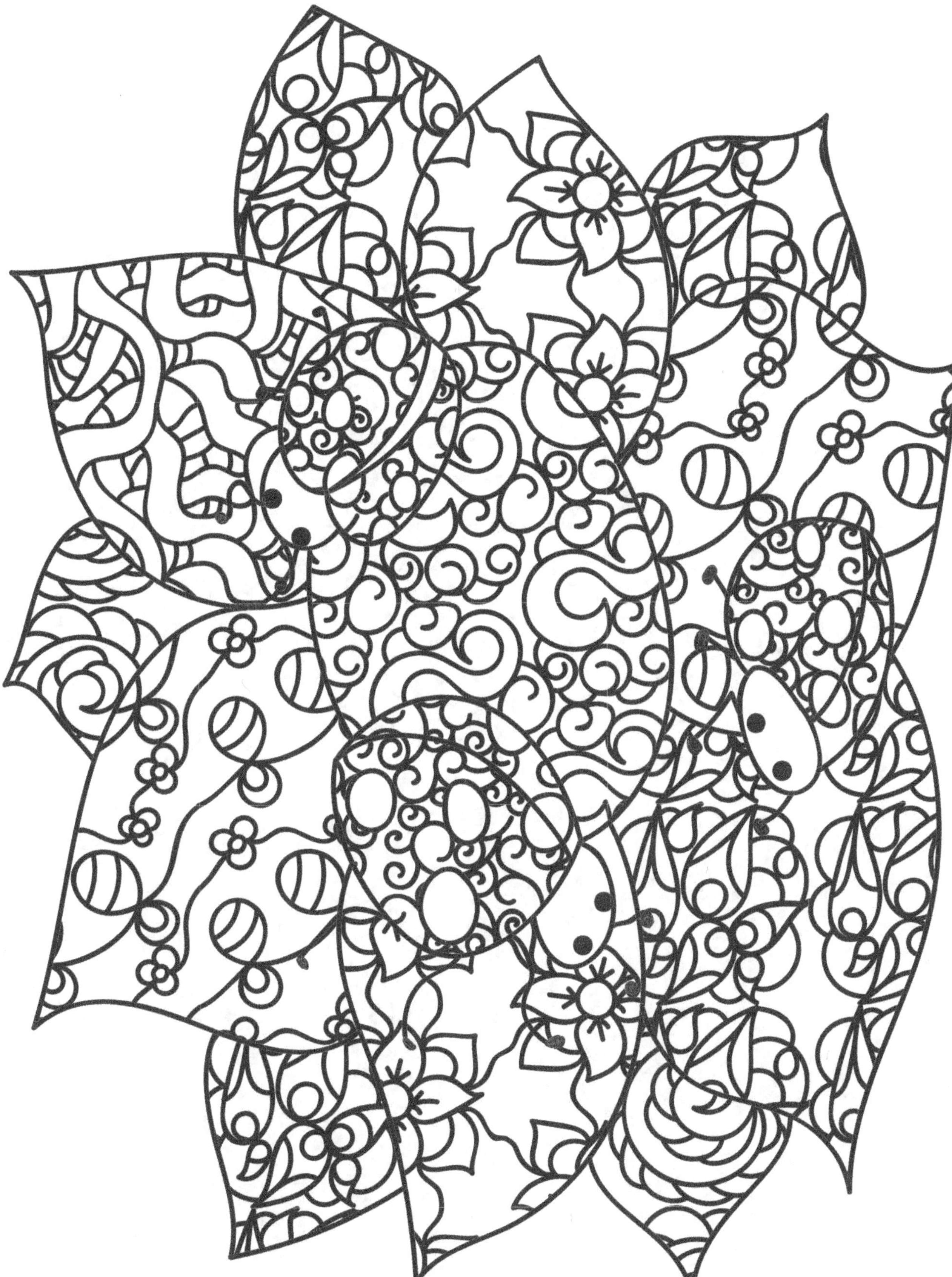

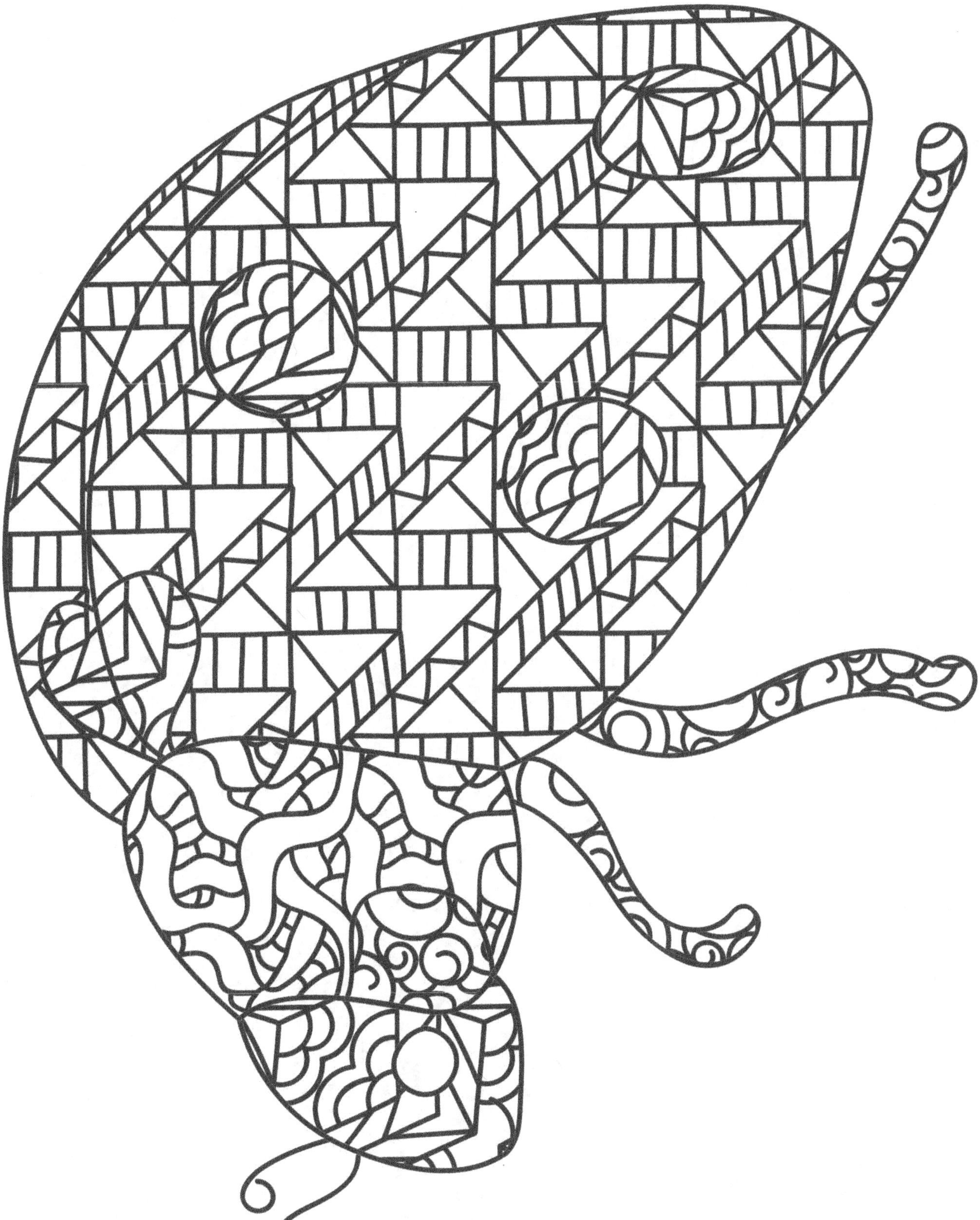

COLOR TEST PAGE

COLOR TEST PAGE

www.ingramcontent.com/pod-product-compliance
Lightning Source LLC
Chambersburg PA
CBHW081244280526
45787CB00006B/2791
* 9 7 8 1 5 4 6 8 3 5 7 6 9 *